Space Explorer

SPACE EQUIPMENT

Patricia Whitehouse

Heinemann Library
Chicago, Illinois

© 2004 Heinemann Library
a division of Reed Elsevier Inc.
Chicago, Illinois

Customer Service 888-454-2279

Visit our website at www.heinemannlibrary.com

Designed by Heinemann Library
Printed in China by South China Printing.

08 07 06 05 04
10 9 8 7 6 5 4 3 2 1

Library of Congress Cataloging-in-Publication Data

Whitehouse, Patricia, 1958-
  Space equipment / Patricia Whitehouse.
     v. cm. -- (Space explorer)
  Includes bibliographical references and index.
  Contents: Equipment for learning -- Telescopes on earth
-- Radio waves from space -- Mission control -- The
launch pad -- Using equipment in space -- Landing the
space shuttle -- Satellites for communication -- How
satellites work -- Global Positioning System -- Photographs
of Earth -- Telescopes in space -- Space probes in the
solar system -- Sojourner lands on Mars -- Amazing space
equipment facts.
  ISBN 1-4034-5154-0 (Library Binding-Hardcover) -- ISBN
1-4034-5658-5 (Paperback)
  1. Astronautics--Equipment and supplies--Juvenile
literature. 2. Space vehicles--Juvenile literature. [1.
Astronautics--Equipment and supplies.] I. Title. II. Series.
  TL793.W49 2004
  629.47--dc22
                                2003026764

Acknowledgements
The author and publishers are grateful to the following for
permission to reproduce copyright material:

Cover photograph: NASA

p. 4 Bo Zaunders/Corbis; p. 5, Photri; p. 6
AURA/NSF/NOAO; p. 7 NASA; p. 8 Jess Alford/Getty
Images/Photodisc; p. 9 Photri; p. 10 NASA; p. 11 ESA; p. 13
NASA; p. 14 NASA; p. 15 Photri; p. 16 James L. Amos,
Peter Arnold Inc/Science Photo Library; p. 17 NASA; p. 18
Matthew Flor, Jason Reed/Getty Images/Photodisc; p. 19
NASA/Topham; p. 21 Science Photo Library; p. 22 Stock
Trek/Getty Images/Photodisc; p. 23 NASA; p. 24
NASA/Science Photo Library; p. 25 H. Richer/NASA; p. 26
NASA/Corbis (royalty free); p. 27 NASA; p. 28 Science
Photo Library; p. 29 NASA, SPL/Science Photo Library

Special thanks to Geza Gyuk of the Adler Planetarium for
his comments in preparation of this book.

Every effort has been made to contact copyright holders
of any material reproduced in this book. Any omissions
will be rectified in subsequent printings if notice is given to
the Publishers.

Some words are shown in bold, **like this.** You can find out
what they mean by looking in the glossary.

Contents

Space Equipment

People use a lot of different equipment to learn about space. Some equipment is on Earth and some is in space.

Astronauts need special equipment
in space.

Astronauts need equipment to get
into space, to live and work there,
and to come home safely.

Telescopes are used to see planets, stars, and other objects in space. Telescopes make objects that are far away look much bigger.

This is a telescope at Kitt Peak National Observatory.

6

Most telescopes are connected to computers. A computer saves the telescope's pictures. **Astronomers** look at these pictures to learn about space.

Radio Telescopes

Astronomers also use radio **telescopes.** Many space objects send out radio waves. Radio telescopes on Earth collect the radio waves.

A radio telescope looks like a very big TV satellite dish. This one is as big as a soccer field.

Astronomers do not listen to radio waves. They send them through a computer to make pictures.

The Space Shuttle

The space shuttle is an important piece of equipment. It takes other pieces of equipment and **astronauts** into space.

The space shuttle has computers, fax machines, and special radios that allow astronauts to talk to Mission Control.

Some of the screens in Mission Control show the space shuttle taking off.

The space shuttle and each piece of equipment on it are checked before liftoff. People at Mission Control use many computers to check on the space shuttle during the mission.

The Launch Pad

Space shuttles take off from a launch pad. A big tractor is used to take the space shuttle to the launch pad.

fuel tank

rocket booster

shuttle

tractor

United States

USA

A special frame holds
the shuttle in place.
It has an elevator so
the **astronauts** can
get up to the shuttle.

launch pad

Equipment in Space

The space shuttle travels around Earth so fast that it is like falling. Everything inside falls, too. It makes **astronauts** and everything in the station float around. This is called weightlessness.

This astronaut is working on a satellite in the cargo bay.

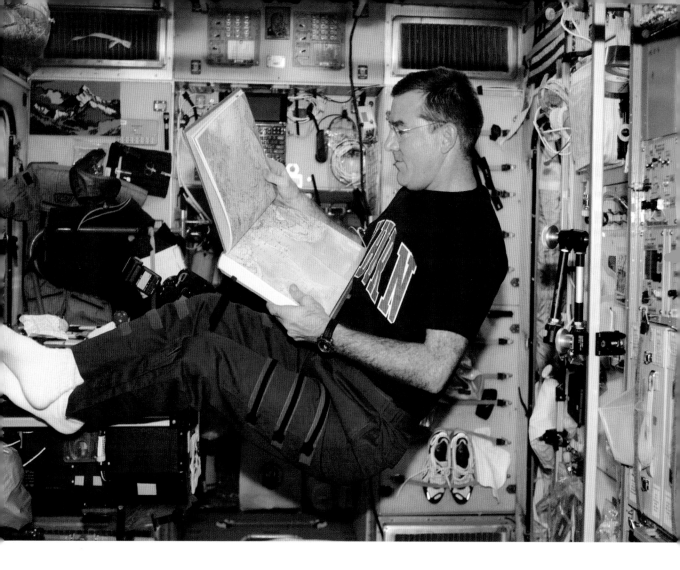

Sometimes small equipment is tied down to keep it from floating away. Other things are stuck to the walls with hook-and-ring fasteners. Bigger equipment must be kept in cupboards.

Shuttle Landing

When the space shuttle returns to Earth, the bottom of the shuttle gets very hot. Special tiles stop the inside of the shuttle from getting hot, too.

The tiles can break or burn off during landing. This person is putting on new tiles.

The shuttle looks like an airplane.
Its shape helps it to land smoothly.
Booster rockets help it change
direction. A parachute helps it to
stop quickly.

parachute

Satellites

A **satellite** is an object that **orbits** a planet. Many satellites orbit Earth. Televisions, telephones, and radios use satellites. Computers link them to the satellites in space.

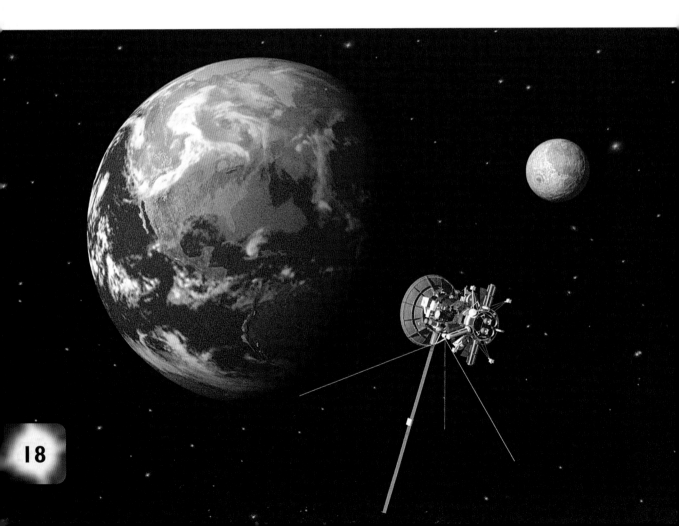

This satellite is being launched
from a space shuttle.

Satellites can be launched into space
from a space shuttle. Some satellites
can orbit Earth in 90 minutes. Others
are much farther away and take a
whole day to orbit Earth.

A television show is recorded in light and sound waves. Computers change them to radio waves. Radio waves are sent to a **satellite** in space. The satellite sends radio waves to satellite dishes on Earth.

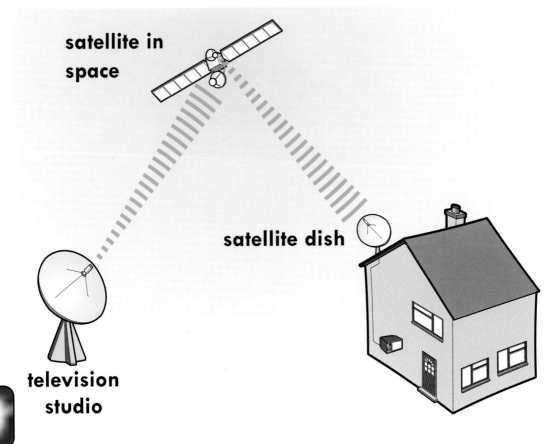

satellite in space

satellite dish

television studio

The satellite dishes send the radio
waves to televisions. The televisions
change the waves back into sound
and light. This is the television show
that you see.

Photographs of Earth

Some **satellites** can take photographs of Earth from space. Some take photographs of changes in weather patterns. **Meteorologists** use these to help them **forecast** the weather.

A satellite in space took this photo of a hurricane.

Mount Everest

Some satellite photographs can show how Earth changes. Satellite photos show that the highest place on Earth, Mount Everest, has grown 6½ feet (2 meters) in 50 years.

Telescopes in Space

In 1990, the Hubble Space **Telescope** was launched into space. **Astronomers** hoped the pictures that it sent to Earth would be very clear.

These astronauts are working on the Hubble Space Telescope while it is tied to the space shuttle.

This is a picture of stars taken by the Hubble Space Telescope.

Many people, such as **astronauts** and astronomers, worked to get the Hubble Space Telescope into space. It has taken many pictures of space for astronomers to study.

Space Probes

Space equipment can travel to places people cannot. Some places are too far away. Some are too dangerous. Pieces of equipment that travel into deep space are called **space probes.**

This is the space probe Voyager I.

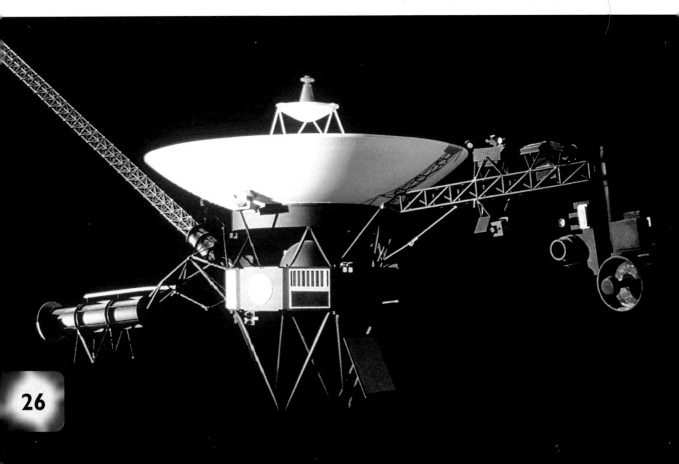

Voyager 1 is a space probe. It was sent into space in 1977 to take pictures of the planets Saturn and Jupiter. It has sent messages back to Earth for over 25 years.

Voyager 1 sent these photographs of Saturn's rings back to Earth.

Probes on Planets

Space probes have landed on the Moon and on the planets Venus and Mars. Pathfinder was a space probe that landed on Mars.

This is a photo of Mars taken by Pathfinder.

The space probe Pathfinder carried a robot called Sojourner. Scientists on Earth sent messages that told the robot where to move. Sojourner then sent photos of Mars back to Earth.

Amazing space facts

 Space shuttles have over 2.5 million parts.

 The biggest **satellite** dish is at Arecibo Observatory, in Puerto Rico. It is 1,000 feet (305 meters) wide.

 The Hubble Space **Telescope orbits** Earth at 17,000 miles (26,900 kilometers) per hour.

 The first telescope was used in 1609, almost 400 years ago.

Glossary

astronaut person who goes into space

astronomer scientist who studies space

forecast guess what is going to happen in the future

gravity force that pulls objects together

meteorologist scientist who studies weather

Mission Control office on Earth where scientists keep in contact with space missions

orbit the path one object makes around another

satellite object that moves around a planet or a moon

space probe spacecraft used to explore space

telescope instrument that makes objects far away seem larger

More Books to Read

Wallace, Karen. *Rockets and Spaceships*. New York: Dorling Kindersley Publishing, 2001.

Whitehouse, Patricia. *Space Travel*. Chicago: Heinemann Library, 2004.

Whitehouse, Patricia. *Working in Space*. Chicago: Heinemann Library, 2004.

Index